Lupita Nyong'o

Actor, Filmmaker, Activist

HEATHER E. SCHWARTZ

LERNER PUBLICATIONS ◆ MINNEAPOLIS

Lerner Publications Company
An imprint of Lerner Publishing Group, Inc.
241 First Avenue North
Minneapolis, MN 55401 USA

For reading levels and more information, look up this title at www.lernerbooks.com.

Image credits: Taylor Hill/Getty Images, p. 2; Kevin Winter/Getty Images, pp. 6, 15; Christopher Polk/Getty Images, p. 8; Wollertz/Shutterstock.com, p. 9; Gotham/WireImage/Getty Images, p. 10; Simon Maina/AFP/Getty Images, p. 12; Walter Bibikow/DigitalVision/Getty Images, p. 13; Astrid Stawiarz/Getty Images, p. 14; Michael Tran/FilmMagic/Getty Images, p. 16; Caleb Holder/Shutterstock.com, p. 18; Ethan Miller/Getty Images, p. 19; George Pimentel/WireImage/Getty Images, p. 20; David M. Benett/Getty Images, p. 21; Larry Busacca/Getty Images, p. 22; Victor Chavez/Getty Images, p. 24; Jemal Countess/Getty Images, p. 25; Tony Karumba/AFP/Getty Images, p. 26; Bruce Glikas/FilmMagic/Getty Images, p. 28; Jenny Anderson/WireImage/Getty Images, p. 29; Alberto E. Rodriguez/Getty Images, p. 30; Isaac Kasamani/AFP/Getty Images, p. 31; GP Images/WireImage/Getty Images, p. 32; lev radin/Shutterstock.com, p. 33; Axelle/Bauer-Griffin/FilmMagic/Getty Images, p. 34; Emma McIntyre/Getty Images, pp. 35, 39; Dan MacMedan/Getty Images, p. 36; Dia Dipasupil/WireImage/Getty Images, p. 37; Raymond Hall/GC Images/Getty Images, p. 38. Cover: Jamie McCarthy/Getty Images.

Main body text set in Rotis Serif Std 55 Regular. Typeface provided by Adobe Systems.

Editor: Shee Yang **Designer:** Lauren Cooper **Photo Editor:** Brianna Kaiser
Lerner team: Sue Marquis

Library of Congress Cataloging-in-Publication Data

Names: Schwartz, Heather E., author.
Title: Lupita Nyong'o : actor, filmmaker, activist / Heather E. Schwartz.
Description: Minneapolis : Lerner Publications, [2022] | Series: Gateway biographies | Includes
    bibliographical references and index. | Audience: Ages: 9–14 | Audience: Grades: 4–6 |
    Summary: "After winning an Oscar for her debut feature film 12 Years a Slave, Lupita
    Nyong'o went from amateur actress to A-list celebrity. Read about Nyong'o's journey and
    how she became a cultural icon"— Provided by publisher.
Identifiers: LCCN 2019055137 (print) | LCCN 2019055138 (ebook) | ISBN 9781541596757 (library
    binding) | ISBN 9781728400310 (ebook)
Subjects: LCSH: Nyong'o, Lupita—Juvenile literature. | Motion picture actors and actresses—
    Kenya—Biography—Juvenile literature. | Women, Black—Kenya—Biography—Juvenile
    literature.
Classification: LCC PN2991.8.N96 S39 2021 (print) | LCC PN2991.8.N96 (ebook) | DDC
    791.4302/8092 [B]—dc23

LC record available at https://lccn.loc.gov/2019055137
LC ebook record available at https://lccn.loc.gov/2019055138

Manufactured in the United States of America
1-47783-48220-4/12/2021

CONTENTS

Lupita Nyong'o accepts the Oscar for Best Actress in a Supporting Role at the Dolby Theatre in Hollywood, California, on March 2, 2014.

Walking on the red carpet to the 2014 Academy Awards, Lupita Nyong'o looked stunning in her sky-blue gown with its pleated floor-length skirt. She told reporters the color reminded her of Nairobi, her hometown in Kenya. It was nice to have a bit of home with her as she navigated the star-studded event. She was there as a nominee for Best Supporting Actress for her portrayal of Patsey in the movie *12 Years a Slave*.

Seated next to her brother, Junior, she listened as the names of the nominees were announced. Her competition included Julia Roberts, Jennifer Lawrence, Sally Hawkins, and June Squibb—all outstanding actors.

Actor Christoph Waltz read the nominees. After hearing "and the Oscar goes to," and her name, Nyong'o put her hand over her face in surprise. She stood, took a breath to compose herself, and hugged her brother. More congratulatory hugs followed, including one from *12 Years a Slave* director Steve McQueen. Holding her golden statue, she stepped up to the microphone shouting, "Yes!"

Nyong'o addresses the media backstage after her acceptance speech.

After thanking the Academy for recognizing her, Nyong'o began her speech with a statement that made it clear that her work was bigger than herself. "It doesn't escape me for one moment that so much joy in my life is thanks to so much pain in someone else's," she said. "And so I want to salute the spirit of Patsey for her guidance."

Nyong'o held back tears. Her voice broke with emotion. "When I look down at this golden statue, may it remind me, and every little child, that no matter where you're from, your dreams are valid."

Only two years before, Nyong'o had been an acting student at Yale University. As an Oscar-winning actor, her fame would allow her to speak out and make a difference on the issues that mattered to her most.

A Mexican Kenyan Childhood

Although Lupita Amondi Nyong'o spent most of her childhood in Kenya, she was born in Mexico City, Mexico, on March 1, 1983. She was the second of six children. Her parents moved back to Kenya when she was one so her father, Peter Anyang Nyong'o, could teach at the University of Nairobi.

Living in the suburbs of Nairobi, Lupita's favorite pastime was playing make believe with her dolls. She also loved attending community plays. Her family was artistic. Her father acted in high school, and her aunt performed in local theater. Lupita was only eight or nine years old when she watched the movie *The Color Purple*.

"It was the first time I'd seen someone like me on screen," Nyong'o said. "Whoopi Goldberg had

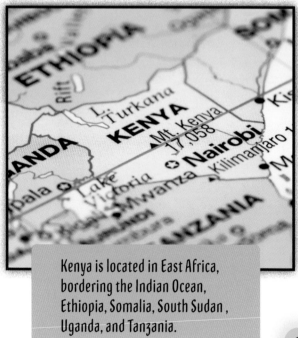

Kenya is located in East Africa, bordering the Indian Ocean, Ethiopia, Somalia, South Sudan , Uganda, and Tanzania.

Alek Wek walks the runway at the 2019 Tommy Hilfiger fashion show in Harlem, New York.

my kind of hair and was dark like me. I thought, maybe I could do this for a living."

More often throughout her childhood, she felt that her skin was too dark. She would later learn that this feeling was due to colorism, the belief that the lighter your skin, the more beautiful you are. Lupita was often bullied by her lighter-skinned peers. Eventually, she felt that she was not beautiful at all. This experience would later motivate her to speak out against colorism worldwide.

As she grew up, another celebrity also inspired her. Model Alek Wek started her modeling career in 1995, when Lupita was twelve. Over the next few years, Lupita watched as the South Sudanese British model was featured in magazines and on runways all

Exploring Her Mexican Roots

When Lupita was sixteen, she moved to Mexico for seven months to learn Spanish. She loved spending time in the country she'd left as a baby, and she also came to love Mexican food and the friends she made. Lupita enjoys learning languages. She speaks English, Swahili, Spanish, and Italian.

over the world. At first Lupita couldn't believe that someone who looked so much like herself was considered beautiful. Lupita had no idea that one day she would also inspire other young girls to follow their own dreams. Exposed to someone who looked like her, Lupita began to redefine what it meant to be beautiful in the world.

When Lupita was fourteen, she made her professional stage debut playing Juliet in *Romeo and Juliet*. Each time Lupita was onstage, she felt as if she came to life. She loved it. But she wasn't quite ready to make acting a career. In her family, it was more common to treat performing as a hobby instead of work.

Embracing Her Dream

By the time Lupita was nineteen, she knew she wanted to be a movie actor. But she was still hesitant to commit to it. Instead, with her family's support, she studied filmmaking and theater at Hampshire College, in Amherst, Massachusetts.

"When I was younger, I was almost too afraid to admit that I wanted to be an actor," Nyong'o later said. "I didn't know any successful actors in Kenya, so I felt like I could get away with going to college to study film more easily than I could with saying, 'I want to be an actor.' That's what I did."

Albinism affects one in twenty thousand people around the world.

She worked on several films as a production assistant. For her senior thesis, she wrote, directed, and produced her own film. *In My Genes* was about albinism, a condition that causes a person's skin, hair, and eyes to have little or no color. Her movie told the stories of eight people living with albinism in Kenya. It was screened at several film festivals and won awards including Best Documentary at the Five College Film Festival in 2008.

The Nyong'os were a wealthy and prestigious family. When Nyong'o graduated from Hampshire College and struggled with what to do next, she was able to take a year to consider her next steps. She spent that time at home in Nairobi. With her family's support, she finally decided to pursue acting professionally.

Yale University is in New Haven, Connecticut.

"I knew that if I didn't try acting, that would be the one thing I would regret, so I decided to apply to acting schools," Nyong'o said. "If I got in, I'd take it as a sign that I should pursue acting as a career. If I didn't get in, I was prepared to figure out some plan B."

Nyong'o applied for her master of fine arts at Yale School of Drama, in New Haven, Connecticut. The school has produced some of the most respected actors, including Meryl Streep, Paul Newman, and Sigourney Weaver. Up against 950 applicants, Nyong'o was selected to join 32 finalists for the acting program. The finalists met with program directors and teachers and auditioned. She joined a class of only sixteen students. She was eager for real acting training that she could rely on when her instincts might not be enough. She wanted to develop technique and felt Yale would be the place to push to the next level.

Just before she left for school, a friend scouting for a Kenyan MTV miniseries asked Nyong'o if she knew of any actors who might like a role. Fully committed to her goal, she had no problem suggesting herself and landed a role on the show *Shuga*. She played a young woman in the drama that brought attention to HIV and AIDS. Nyong'o was pleased to use her artistic work for awareness and change that she believed in. Her role led her to become an HIV and AIDS activist in real life.

"*Shuga* was so effective on Kenyan youth because of the fact that it was modern, it was hip, it was fast and

Nyong'o attends a campaign to defeat AIDS and other illnesses on May 30, 2013.

furious," Nyong'o said at the time. "In *Shuga*, it's young people telling young people, advising young people. So I think that is very effective and young people respond to that."

At Yale, most days began at nine in the morning. Her schedule was packed with classes, rehearsals, and shows that sometimes went on until eleven at night. Her classmates became her close friends. They spent holidays and birthdays together, including a birthday party Nyong'o hosted for herself at an African restaurant.

Just before completing her master's degree, Nyong'o landed an audition for a role in *12 Years a Slave*. Based on an autobiography, the movie takes place before the American Civil War (1861–1865) and tells the story of Solomon Northup, a free Black man who was kidnapped and sold into slavery for twelve years. During that time, he meets Patsey, an enslaved person born into captivity who faced horrible abuse.

Some of the cast and crew of *12 Years a Slave* pose during the Golden Globe Awards on January 12, 2014.

Her First Feature Film

In 2012 Nyong'o traveled to Los Angeles, California, to meet with *12 Years a Slave*'s casting director, Francine Maisler. She created an audition meant to showcase Nyong'o's ability to express suffering.

"She asked me to kneel down and then she would yell at me like a drill sergeant, 'Start from there! Go back! Start from the beginning!'" Nyong'o said. "I would start off at one level of despair and from there it was all downhill. Then she would start me off again at that lowest point and demand I go even lower."

The role she was auditioning for would be emotional and difficult. But that was exactly why Nyong'o had gotten her master's degree. She was talented, trained, and ready for the challenge.

For his contribution to the arts, Steve McQueen was knighted by Queen Elizabeth, officially changing his title to Sir Steve McQueen.

Nyong'o had a second audition with McQueen. The next day, she received a phone call from him offering her the role of Patsey.

"My knees gave way and I sat on the pavement," she said later. "It was so crazy."

When she realized she was going to be working with actors such as Brad Pitt and Michael Fassbender, Nyong'o was intimidated. But when her father congratulated her on getting the job, she realized that was how she had to think of it: as a job she had to do.

Nyong'o went to Yale to learn technique and now more than ever, she felt the value of her education. She was confident and prepared to take on the role of Patsey. She knew she was as ready as she'd ever be.

She began tackling her new role by reading the autobiography of Solomon Northup and learning details about Patsey's childhood as an enslaved person. She came up with the idea to have Patsey make corn dolls in the movie.

"I felt she was robbed of her childhood and I wanted to find ways of capturing that sensibility," she said. "I learnt how to make the dolls, and made one almost every day. It was a therapeutic thing for Patsey, a way to stay in the zone, a part of her that couldn't be enslaved."

Nyong'o visited the National Great Blacks in Wax Museum, in Baltimore, Maryland. There, she noted the size of a 500-pound (227 kg) bale of cotton on display. Patsey was valued for her ability to pick that much cotton in a single day. Most people could only pick half as much.

A bale of cotton like the one shown here weighs about 500 pounds (227 kg), as much as Patsey picked in a day.

When the movie began shooting, Nyong'o empathized with Patsey so much that she had trouble sleeping, especially one night when she had to go to bed wearing prosthetic welts on her back so she'd be ready for filming the next day.

"I could only sleep on my stomach and I was so uncomfortable and haunted by these 'wounds,'" she said. "I realized my night of discomfort was temporary. Hers was permanent. It broke my heart realizing how she had zero choice."

Getting close to Patsey was part of the job, but Nyong'o knew it was also important to take care of herself. Between takes, she broke character and made sure she was herself again. She also had a strong, positive working relationship with Fassbender, who played Patsey's enslaver and abuser in the film. They shot many scenes together in which Fassbender was cruel and abusive. But they always took steps to make sure they were both doing okay. Before and after each scene, they made eye contact, squeezed each other's hands, and hugged.

An Award-Winning Film

After *12 Years a Slave* was released, it was honored with several awards, including the Academy Award for Best Picture and the Golden Globe Award for Best Picture. Nyong'o won several awards of her own, including the Academy Award for Best Actress in a Supporting Role, the Screen Actors Guild Award for Outstanding Performance by a Female Actor, and the National Association for the Advancement of Colored People (NAACP) Image Award for Outstanding Supporting Actress in a Motion Picture.

Nyong'o poses with her Outstanding Performance award from the Screen Actors Guild.

Nyong'o expressed that they needed each other's support, especially when completing difficult scenes.

Star Power

Her performance in *12 Years a Slave* catapulted her career. Suddenly, she was a well-known, in-demand

Fassbender and Nyong'o became good friends following their intense scenes in *12 Years a Slave*.

actress. The challenge was clear as she set out to follow her own breakout success.

"The bar has been set very high externally and internally. But I don't want to feed into that pressure of expectation," she said. "[The movie] was so fulfilling and artistic. I've tasted that and I obviously want to experience that kind of creative fulfillment again, but I also know that I can't replicate that. I want a varied acting experience and that may include some failure and that's healthy."

In her next film, Nyong'o played a flight attendant in *Non-Stop*, a thriller about a plane full of passengers whose lives are threatened by an on-flight killer. It wasn't a starring role, but she learned a lot working on the movie. Filming mostly in an indoor studio was a new experience. Nyong'o was grateful to learn from other professionals in the cast, including Liam Neeson and Julianne Moore.

"It was what I needed to do," she said. "It was the perfect antidote to *12 Years a Slave.* It was a different genre with different demands. It was very technical and fun."

Along with being recognized for her talent, Nyong'o received a flood of attention for her beauty. The world of high fashion embraced her. She was featured on the cover of *Vogue* in 2014 (and several times after that). She became an ambassador for the beauty brand Lancôme and was later featured in a campaign by the Italian fashion brand Miu Miu alongside A-list actors Elle Fanning, Elizabeth Olsen, and Bella Heathcote.

Left to right: Lancôme ambassadors Julia Roberts, Isabella Rossellini, Nyong'o, Penelope Cruz, and Lily Collins attend the company's eightieth anniversary party in Paris, France.

Nyong'o poses in a portrait booth at the 2013 Toronto International Film Festival.

Nyong'o had never cared much for fashion. One day as she was putting on a beaded dress, she cried thinking about all the people who'd worked so hard to create it. Becoming a fashion icon had never been part of her plans. The most exciting thing about her career wasn't the fame. She cared much more about the chance to grow as a person.

"I always love to learn new things. That's the reason I like being an actor. I want to have a varied human experience, to do things outside of my comfort zone," she explained. "I want to be uncomfortable—acting is uncomfortable. I'm interested in doing things that terrify me."

Another benefit to her growing career was her ability to inspire others. In 2014 *People* magazine named her its Most Beautiful Person. She used the opportunity to speak out about her experiences growing up, seeing people who looked different from her portrayed as the most beautiful on television.

Lending Her Support

In 2014 Nyong'o got involved in a cause she felt connected to after playing the role of an enslaved person. A minor-league baseball stadium was at the center of a land-use controversy in Shockoe Bottom, a neighborhood in Richmond, Virginia. While some felt it would be good for the city, many others believed it would only hide a shameful past. Before the Civil War, the city had served as a major hub in the trade of enslaved people. More than three hundred thousand people had been bought and sold there.

The National Trust for Historic Preservation led a campaign to oppose the stadium. The trust asked for Nyong'o's help, and she used social media to post a letter to the town's mayor.

"The tactic of the enslaver was to systematically erase all memory of the African's past; let us not repeat this ill by contributing to the erasure of his past in America too," she wrote. "Though this history is ugly and unjust, Shockoe Bottom is a site of conscience, a place where we can bear witness to the human rights abuses of slavery, learn from the lessons of history, and spark a conscience in people so that they can choose the actions that promote justice and lasting peace today."

Her words reached not only the mayor but close to four million followers, helping to halt the project and focus on developing a heritage museum honoring enslaved people in Shockoe Bottom.

"Light skin and long, flowing, straight hair. Subconsciously you start to appreciate those things more than what you possess," she said later. "I was happy for all the girls who would see me on (the cover) and feel a little more seen."

Return to the Stage

Fame and fashion were fun, but they were not the focus for Nyong'o. Her ambition was to be a good actress, and she continued challenging herself with new roles.

Costars Oscar Isaac and Nyong'o at the premiere of *Star Wars: The Force Awakens.*

"For me, I love to take on roles that require me to learn something new and really challenge my understanding of what it takes to be a successful human being," she said. "In that sense, I guess I am drawn to really hard material."

In 2015 she was excited to play the animated character Maz Kanata in *Star*

Wars: The Force Awakens. While the audience heard her voice, they never saw her body.

"There was a liberation in being able to play in a medium where my body was not the thing in question," she said. "The acting challenge I was looking for was completely different, a complete departure from *12 Years a Slave.*"

Nyong'o also longed to return to the stage. During her graduate study at Yale, she'd been an understudy in the play *Eclipsed.* She had been moved by the story, which told of five women struggling to survive in captivity in war-torn Liberia. Nyong'o starred in an off-Broadway run of the play in 2015. Nyong'o played the role of a fifteen-year-old girl.

Nyong'o [*left*] and Pascale Armand in character during the opening night of *Eclipsed.*

"I feel extremely grateful to find myself in the position that I find myself, and I use the little weight that I have in order to do passion projects and in order to tell stories that otherwise would not be told," she said. "I also recognize that in the position I'm in, I have the rare privilege of choice as an actress—choice, and the ability in the room to make decisions, which is something that I don't take lightly. It's something that I really value, and something that I recognize as exceptional."

As busy as she was, Nyong'o continued with causes she believed in. She began working with WildAid as a global elephant ambassador in 2015, encouraging people to learn about elephants. She visited an elephant orphanage in Nairobi and spoke out in favor of a worldwide ban on the sale of ivory. With her support, the

Nyong'o returns home to Kenya to kick-start a new campaign to stop the slaughter of elephants for ivory.

organization promoted her trip on TV, social media, and radio, as well as in newspapers and magazines and on billboards. She was using her platform in valuable ways.

Oscar Controversy

In January 2016, the Academy Awards were just around the corner. With the nominations in, many were outraged. Although the pool of amazing performances by wonderful actors was very diverse, it was the second year in a row that only white actors had been nominated. Several movies had been written and directed by people of color. Yet only white people who'd worked on the films were in the running for writing and directing awards. The Academy's choices seemed deliberate and discriminatory.

Many actors spoke out in protest, and Nyong'o was one of them. She expressed her disappointment over the lack of diversity among the Oscar nominees. She also used the moment to move the conversation in a direction that could create change.

"I'm happy that this conversation is happening, because inclusion only happens when we're all aware that it needs to happen," she said. "Otherwise things cannot change, if they're not brought to the fore. This is a conversation that has been happening for a long time, and right now it has a fuel that I hope can only result in an expansion of the imagination when it comes to what stories are viable to be told."

Facing Forward

Throughout 2016 Nyong'o continued to find new challenges for herself as an artist. In March her star power helped take the play *Eclipsed* from off-Broadway to Broadway. For the first time, a Broadway play had a female playwright, a female director, and an all-female cast. It was nominated for six Tony Awards and won Best Costume Design of a Play. Nyong'o was pleased to be part of a show that brought to life dramatic, important material based on real events.

Eclipsed playwright Danai Gurira (*left*) and Nyong'o also star together in Marvel's *Black Panther.*

"[You] may not have known anything (about Liberia or its civil war) when it begins, but the play welcomes you into this compound. You learn something very deep. You're shocked, your mind is open, and your

Left to right: Liesl Tommy, Gurira, Nyong'o, Pascale Armand, and Akosua Busia during an *Eclipsed* curtain call

heart is broken. Where you may have known facts, now you have feelings," Nyong'o said.

Her work on the play inspired her to begin working with Mother Health International in April 2016. The organization helps women and children in Uganda and other war-torn areas by creating birthing centers. Nyong'o spoke out about the parallels she saw between the play and the real events happening in Uganda.

"As an actor, it's a privilege to be able to shed light on issues that are relevant to the world we live in today," she said. "With *Eclipsed*, hopefully what we're doing is putting emotion behind hard facts, so that people who experience this play can then encounter an organization like Mother Health International and have an emotional attachment to what it is that they're doing. Out of that, I think, comes real, effective change."

In April she voiced Raksha in the animated film *The Jungle Book*. It was her first voice-over role for an animated movie. She was excited to play a wolf mother to a human. Even though she didn't have children of her own, she'd always loved children. She knew she could find her way into the character. Nyong'o channeled her own mother, who she describes as fierce and firm in her motherly ways.

Later that year, Nyong'o had another chance to play a fierce mother in the Disney movie *Queen of Katwe*. As Harriet, she was a single parent to main character Phiona, a fifteen-year old Ugandan

Nyong'o poses with her on-screen son, Neel Sethi, at the world premiere of *The Jungle Book*.

chess prodigy. She was particularly excited by the project because it was a true story about an African family trying to find a way to reach big dreams.

The movie was filmed in Katwe, Uganda, a large neighborhood where Phiona grew up. Nyong'o met the real Harriet when she arrived. She spent time with Harriet, so Nyong'o could learn how to create an authentic version on-screen. While filming in Katwe, Nyong'o said, "For me it was research shooting there, jumping over open sewers, navigating rickety bridges. Your life is in danger. It was a constant reminder of what Harriet has to contend with and protect her children from."

Left to right: Chess prodigy Phiona Mutesi, filmmaker Mira Nair, Nyong'o, and Phiona's chess coach, Robert Katende, get together in Kampala, Uganda, on March 28, 2015.

Nyong'o at the *Queen of Katwe* premiere during the 2016 Toronto International Film Festival.

Many of her movie choices were about telling other people's stories and giving them a voice. But at the end of 2017, Nyong'o found herself using her platform in a more personal way. She had her own experiences that needed to be aired so she could help others.

In the fall of 2017, movie producer Harvey Weinstein had been accused by many women in Hollywood of sexual harassment. Soon after, Nyong'o wrote a piece for the *New York Times* stating that she shared a similar experience with Weinstein as the other women who have come forward.

"I felt uncomfortable in my silence, and I wanted to liberate myself from it and contribute to the discussion," she wrote. "That was just what I felt I needed to do, quite viscerally. I couldn't sleep. I needed to get it out."

On January 6, 2020, protesters lined up outside of New York's criminal court to show support for survivors of sexual assault.

The following month, Nyong'o was in the news again. This time, she spoke out when the magazine *Grazia UK* airbrushed her cover photo. It was no small matter. Nyong'o's natural hair was edited and smoothed, making her look more European. The photo changed how she looked. Nyong'o felt that by removing her natural hair texture, the magazine was further spreading the practice of colorism, something she had a personal conflict with.

"As I have made clear so often in the past with every fiber of my being, I embrace my natural heritage and despite having grown up thinking light skin and straight, silky hair were the standards of beauty, I now know that my dark skin and kinky, coily hair are beautiful too," she wrote. "Being featured on the cover of a magazine fulfills me as it is an opportunity to show other dark, kinky-haired people, and particularly our children, that they are beautiful just the way they are."

Nyong'o is proud of her hair and often wears a natural look.

Into the Future

As she continued building her career, Nyong'o plotted her path carefully. She looked for projects that told stories from new perspectives and also gave her a chance to stretch and strengthen her skills. In 2018 she starred in the highly anticipated *Black Panther*, a Marvel superhero film. The story line felt important to her because of the way it empowered and uplifted women.

Nyong'o poses with fans at the world premiere of *Black Panther* at the Dolby Theatre in Hollywood. The movie is the highest-earning solo superhero film in history.

Black Panther cast members (*from left to right*) Angela Bassett, Nyong'o, and Gurira display the Wakanda salute after winning Outstanding Performance by a Cast at the Screen Actor's Guild Awards.

"In *Black Panther*, women belong to a society that recognizes their power and that supports it," Nyong'o said. "Women are not fighting against a power dynamic that puts them in a position of disadvantage. They're part of a society that recognizes they have something to offer and allows them to realize it. And them assuming their power in no way diminishes the men or the Black Panther's power. It's an idyllic image; it's the world as it could be."

In 2019 she starred in Jordan Peele's *Us*, choosing the project in part because the script scared her. To prepare, she watched ten horror films that gave her a sense of the genre's style. The bigger challenge was her role. She played two characters who shared the same physical appearance but lived very different lives.

Later that year, she did another scary movie, this time with a comic twist. In *Little Monsters*, Nyong'o played a kindergarten teacher leading her students to safety through a zombie attack. Working with children came naturally to her. Throughout filming, they called her by her character's name and she acted as a leader even when the cameras weren't rolling.

Nyong'o created a chant that she and the entire cast would do. It was a good way to build community on set in addition to lightening up the atmosphere.

That year Nyong'o wrote a children's book, *Sulwe*. It told a story based on her

Director Jordan Peele (*left*) poses with Nyong'o and her on-screen husband, Winston Duke, at the premiere of *Us* in New York City.

own childhood experiences. It was about a girl with dark skin who learns that she was born beautiful. Nyong'o also became an ambassador for Watch Hunger Stop, an initiative started by designer Michael Kors to raise funds and awareness about world hunger.

Nyong'o shows off her children's book debut, *Sulwe*.

Since Nyong'o's first feature film in 2011, her career has exploded with opportunities, and it hasn't slowed down. At the end of 2019, she appeared in another *Star Wars* film, *Star Wars: The Rise of Skywalker*. She will also appear in the movie based on Trevor Noah's best-selling autobiography *Born a Crime*. It tells the story of Noah's childhood in apartheid South Africa, a time when interracial relationships were illegal. Nyong'o will play Patricia, Noah's mother.

Early in 2021 it was announced that *Sulwe* would be made into an animated musical. Nyong'o read her bestselling book for Netflix's *Bookmarks*, which showcased books by Black authors. Netflix loved the story and decided to create an animated musical based on it.

Then Nyong'o did a twist on an old classic. She joined the cast of *Romeo y Julieta*. The audio performance was based on a Spanish translation of *Romeo and Juliet*. As Julieta, Nyong'o performed alongside award-winning actor Juan Castano.

Nyong'o is taking on a new challenge, the small screen. She will perform alongside superstar Natalie Portman in the television show *Lady in the Lake*. Set in 1960s Baltimore, Nyong'o plays the role of Cleo Sherwood, a woman trying to create more opportunities for Black people. Nyong'o has no intention of holding back in her performances or when she speaks out about important issues.

On January 20, 2018, Nyong'o was a featured speaker at the Los Angeles Women's March, part of a worldwide protest in defense of women's rights.

IMPORTANT DATES

1983	Lupita Amondi Nyong'o is born on March 1, in Mexico City, Mexico.
1984	Her family moves to Kenya.
2007	She graduates from Hampshire College, in Amherst, Massachusetts, with a degree in film and theater studies.
2009	She lands a role on the Kenyan show *Shuga*.
2012	She stars as Patsey in her first feature film, *12 Years a Slave*.
	She graduates from Yale School of Drama with a master's degree.
2014	Nyong'o earns an Oscar for Best Supporting Actress for *12 Years a Slave*, and it receives several other awards.
2015	Nyong'o stars in the movie *Star Wars: The Force Awakens* and returns to the stage in the off-Broadway play *Eclipsed*.
2016	*Eclipsed* moves to Broadway.
	Nyong'o also stars in *The Jungle Book* and *Queen of Katwe,* and begins working with Mother Health International.

2017	Nyong'o speaks out about harassment in Hollywood and the spread of colorism in beauty magazines.
2018	Nyong'o stars in *Black Panther*.
2019	She stars in *Us* and *Little Monsters* and releases her first book, *Sulwe*.
2020	Nyong'o stars in HBO's drama *Americanah*—adapted from the *New York Times* best-selling book of the same name.
2021	She stars in *Romeo y Julieta*.

SOURCE NOTES

8   "Lupita Nyong'o Winning Best Supporting Actress," YouTube video, 3:34, posted by Oscars, March 11, 2014, https://www.youtube.com/watch?v=73fz_uK-vhs.

8   "Lupita."

8   "Lupita."

9–10   Sally Williams, "Lupita Nyong'o: Interview with a Rising Star," *Telegraph* (London), January 10, 2014, https://www.telegraph.co.uk/culture/film /starsandstories/10558449/Lupita-Nyongo-interview -with-a-rising-star.html.

12   T. Cole Rachel, "Lupita Nyong'o," *Interview*, November 5, 2013, https://www.interviewmagazine.com/film /lupita-nyongo.

13   Rachel, "Lupita Nyong'o."

14–15   Mario, "Lupita Nyong'o on Her Role in *Shuga*," MTV, January 20, 2014, http://www.mtvstayingalive.org /blog/2014/01/lupita-nyongo-on-role-in-shuga/.

16   Williams, "Lupita Nyong'o."

17   Williams.

17   Williams.

18   Williams.

20   Jessica Herndon, "Lupita Nyong'o: Hollywood's New Fixation," *Associated Press*, February 18, 2014, https://www.dailyherald.com/article/20140224 /entlife/140229342/.

21 Herndon.

22 Elysa Gardner, "From Kenya (via Yale) with Style: Film's Lupita Nyong'o," *USA Today*, February 8, 2014, https://www.usatoday.com/story/life/movies/2014/02/08/oscar-nominee-lupita-nyongo-discusses-her-amazing-journey/5080445/.

23 Bryan Devasher, "*12 Years a Slave* Actress Lupita Nyong'o Urges Richmond Mayor Dwight Jones to Withdraw Support for Shockoe Ballpark," *Richmond Times-Dispatch*, October 19, 2014, https://www.richmond.com/news/local/years-a-slave-actress-lupita-nyong-o-urges-richmond-mayor/article_775c7fa4-8312-5cca-9d6b-9719fcb546bb.html.

24 Julie Jordan and Antoinette Y. Coulton, "Lupita Nyong'o Is People's Most Beautiful," *People*, April 23, 2014, https://people.com/celebrity/lupita-nyongo-is-peoples-most-beautiful-2/.

24 Olivia Clement, "Lupita Nyong'o Is Rediscovering 'Normalcy,'" *Playbill*, October 16, 2015, http://www.playbill.com/news/article/lupita-nyongo-on-her-bold-ny-stage-debut-ellens-famous-oscar-selfie-and-rediscovering-normalcy-366832.

25 Kelley L. Carter, "Why Lupita Nyong'o Didn't Want to Be Seen in *Star Wars*," BuzzFeed News, December 13, 2015, https://www.buzzfeednews.com/article/kelleylcarter/lupita-nyongo-didnt-want-you-to-see-her-face-in-star-wars.

26 Gordon Cox, "Lupita Nyong'o on Oscars Controversy: 'I'm More Interested in What Is Possible,'" *Variety*, February 4, 2016, https://variety.com/2016/film/news/lupita-nyongo-oscars-diversity-controversy-1201697371/.

27 Cox.

28–29   Sara Vilkomerson, "Lupita Nyong'o, Danai Gurira on Making Broadway History with *Eclipsed*," *Entertainment Weekly*, February 26, 2016, https://ew.com/article/2016/02/26/lupita-nyongo-danai-gurira-ew/.

29–30   Gordon Cox, "Lupita Nyong'o Backs Mother Health Intl. for African Relief," *Variety*, April 5, 2016, https://variety.com/2016/film/news/lupita-nyongo-mother-health-intl-africa-1201745417/.

31   Anne Thompson, "Lupita Nyong'o Finds Her Strength in *Queen of Katwe*," IndieWire, September 28, 2016, https://www.indiewire.com/2016/09/lupita-nyongo-oscar-queen-of-katwe-video-1201730707/.

32   Anna Menta, "Lupita Nyong'o on Her Harvey Weinstein Accusation: 'I Needed to Get It Out,'" *Newsweek*, January 25, 2018, https://www.newsweek.com/lupita-nyongo-harvey-weinstein-accusation-i-needed-get-it-out-791338.

33–34   Helena Horton, "Oscar Winner Lupita Nyong'o Hits Out at *Grazia* Magazine over 'Eurocentric' Airbrush Hairstyle," *Telegraph* (London), November 10, 2017, https://www.telegraph.co.uk/news/2017/11/10/lupita-nyongo-criticises-grazia-airbrushing-photoshoot/.

36   Ella Alexander, "*Black Panther*: Lupita Nyong'o and Danai Gurira on How the Latest Marvel Film Smashes Stereotypes," *Harper's Bazaar*, February 9, 2018, https://www.harpersbazaar.com/uk/culture/culture-news/a16799080/black-panther-lupita-nyongo-danai-gurira-interview/.

SELECTED BIBLIOGRAPHY

Chval, Lauren. "Interview: Lupita Nyong'o on *Queen of Katwe* and Diversifying Hollywood." *Chicago Tribune*, September 19, 2016. https://www.chicagotribune.com/redeye/redeye -interview-lupita-nyongo-queen-of-katwe-20160916-story .html.

Devasher, Bryan. "*12 Years a Slave* Actress Lupita Nyong'o Urges Richmond Mayor Dwight Jones to Withdraw Support for Shockoe Ballpark." *Richmond Times-Dispatch*, October 19, 2014. https://www.richmond.com/news/local/years -a-slave-actress-lupita-nyong-o-urges-richmond-mayor /article_775c7fa4-8312-5cca-9d6b-9719fcb546bb.html.

Galloway, Stephen. "Lupita Nyong'o: From Political Exile to Oscar to Marvel's *Black Panther*." *Hollywood Reporter*, January 25, 2018. https://www.hollywoodreporter.com /features/lupita-nyongo-political-exile-oscar-marvels-black -panther-1077849.

Gardner, Elysa. "From Kenya (via Yale) with Style: Film's Lupita Nyong'o." *USA Today*, February 8, 2014. https://www .usatoday.com/story/life/movies/2014/02/08/oscar-nominee -lupita-nyongo-discusses-her-amazing-journey/5080445/.

Hiatt, Brian. "Lupita Nyong'o on the Mysteries of Jordan Peele's *Us*." *Rolling Stone*, January 31, 2019. https://www .rollingstone.com/movies/movie-features/lupita-nyongo -interview-jordan-peele-us-786635/.

"Lupita Nyong'o's Oscars Gown Takes Twitter by Storm." *Extra*, March 2, 2014. https://extratv.com/2014/03/02/oscars-red -carpet-fashion-lupita-nyongo-nairobi-blue-gown-takes -twitter-by-storm/.

Romano, Tricia. "What Did Lupita Nyong'o's Classmates at Yale Think of Her?" Daily Beast. Last modified July 12, 2017. https://www.thedailybeast.com/what-did-lupita -nyongos-classmates-at-yale-think-of-her.

Shepherd, Jack. "Oscars 2016: Everyone Who Boycotted Academy Awards and Why, from Jada Pinkett Smith to Spike Lee." *Independent* (London), February 28, 2016. https://www.independent.co.uk/arts-entertainment/films /news/oscars-2016-everyone-boycotting-the-academy -awards-and-why-from-jada-pinkett-smith-to-spike -lee-a6902121.html.

Wilson, Julee. "Lupita Nyong'o Stars in Miu Miu Spring 2014 Campaign, We're Not Surprised." HuffPost. Last modified December 6, 2017. https://www.huffpost.com/entry/lupita -nyongo-miu-miu-spring-2014_n_4574800.

Yuan, Jada. "Lupita Nyong'o on *12 Years a Slave*, Getting into Character, and 'Imposter Syndrome.'" Vulture, October 2, 2013. https://www.vulture.com/2013/10/lupita-nyongo-on -12-years-a-slave.html.

FURTHER READING

Books

Harrison, Vashti. *Little Leaders: Bold Women in Black History*. New York: Little, Brown Books for Young People, 2017.
Learn more about Nyong'o and other bold leaders.

Nyong'o, Lupita. *Sulwe*. New York: Simon and Schuster Books for Young Readers, 2019.
Read Nyong'o's picture book based on her own childhood experiences.

Shea, Therese. *Lupita Nyong'o: Oscar-Winning Actress*. Berkeley Heights, NJ, 2019.
Learn more about Nyong'o's path to stardom.

Williams, Alicia. *Genesis Begins Again*. New York: Atheneum, 2019.
Learn more about skin pigmentation and colorism.

Websites

African Wildlife Foundation
https://www.awf.org/
Learn more about a charity that Nyong'o supports.

Lupita Nyong'o
https://www.imdb.com/name/nm2143282/
See what projects Nyong'o has coming up!

Yale School of Drama
https://www.drama.yale.edu/
Learn about the school where Nyong'o studied acting.

INDEX